Nature's Super Secrets

# Why Do Seasons Change?

By Ryan Stark

 Gareth Stevens
Publishing

Please visit our website, www.garethstevens.com. For a free color catalog of all our high-quality books, call toll free 1-800-542-2595 or fax 1-877-542-2596.

Library of Congress Cataloging-in-Publication Data

Stark, Ryan, 1984-
        Why do seasons change? / by Ryan Stark.
cm. – (Nature's super secrets)
Includes bibliographical references and index.
Summary: Brief text and photographs tell about the different seasons and how the changing position of the Earth around the sun gives us four seasons.
Contents: Our changing seasons – Earth's orbit – Spring – Summer – Fall – Winter.
ISBN 978-1-4339-8186-9 (pbk.)
ISBN 978-1-4339-8187-6 (6-pack)
ISBN 978-1-4339-8185-2 (hard bound)
1. Seasons—Juvenile literature    [1. Seasons]    I. Title
        2013
508.2—dc23

Published in 2013 by
**Gareth Stevens Publishing**
111 East 14th Street, Suite 349
New York, NY 10003

Designer: Nicholas Domiano
Editor: Sarah Machajewski

Photo credits: Cover, p. 1 Elena Blokhina/Shutterstock.com; p. 5 photobank.kiev.ua/Shutterstock.com; p. 7 Evstigneev Alexander/Shutterstock.com; p. 9 Matthew Cole/Shutterstock.com; p. 11 Dorling Kindersley/Getty Images; p. 13 Aleksandr Kurganov/Shutterstock.com; p. 15 Efired/Shutterstock.com; p. 17 S.Borisov/Shutterstock.com;
p. 19 Kotenko Oleksandr/Shutterstock.com; p. 21 (Earth) Alex Staroseltsev/Shutterstock.com; p. (stars) 21 Tjefferson/Shutterstock.com.

Printed in the United States of America

CPSIA compliance information: Batch #CW13GS: For further information contact Gareth Stevens, New York, New York at 1-800-542-2595.

# Contents

**Boldface** words appear in the glossary.

# Our Changing Seasons

We have four seasons on Earth. They are spring, summer, fall, and winter. Some parts of the world have all the seasons, while others stay warm or cold all year long. Do you know what makes the seasons change?

Seasons change because Earth's **axis** is **tilted**. The tilt makes one part of Earth point toward the sun, while the other part points away from it. This causes some parts of Earth to have less sun and warmth than others.

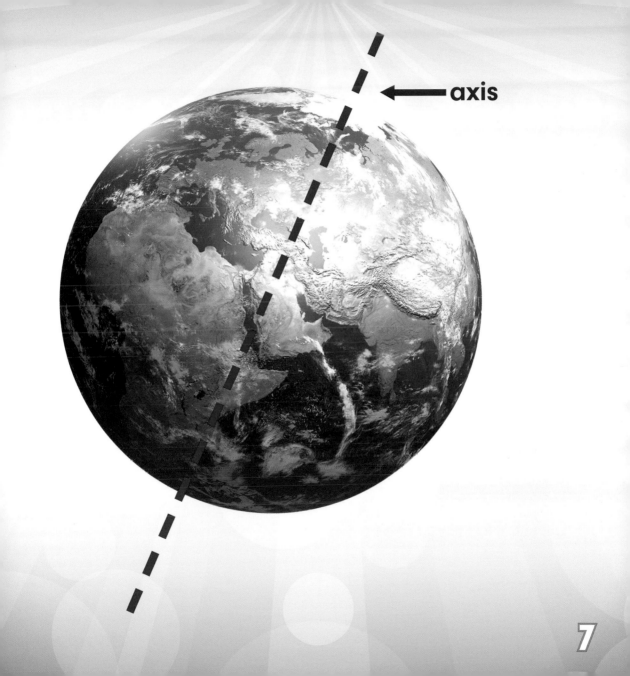

axis

# Earth's Orbit

For part of the year, the top half of Earth tips toward the sun, while the bottom half points away. This changes as Earth moves through its **orbit**! Orbiting makes Earth face the sun from different **positions**.

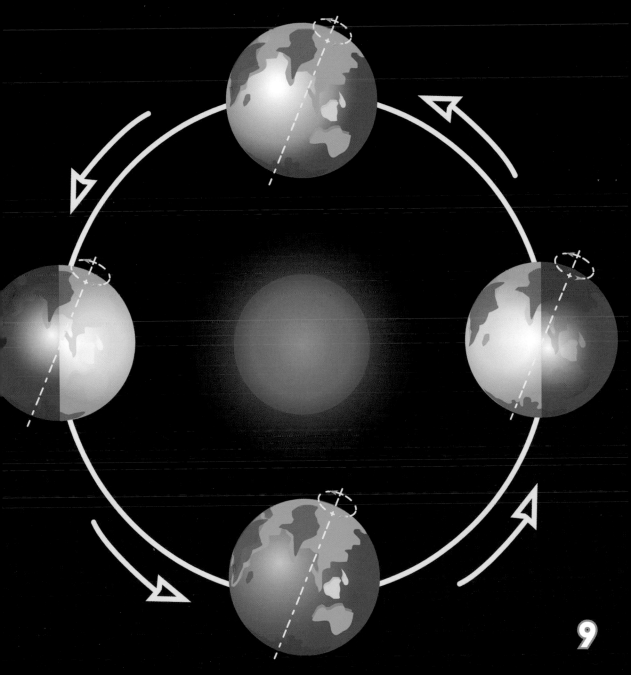

It takes 1 year for Earth to finish its orbit. The changing position of Earth around the sun gives us four seasons. Each season has something that makes it special. If you pay attention, you can see and feel the seasons change.

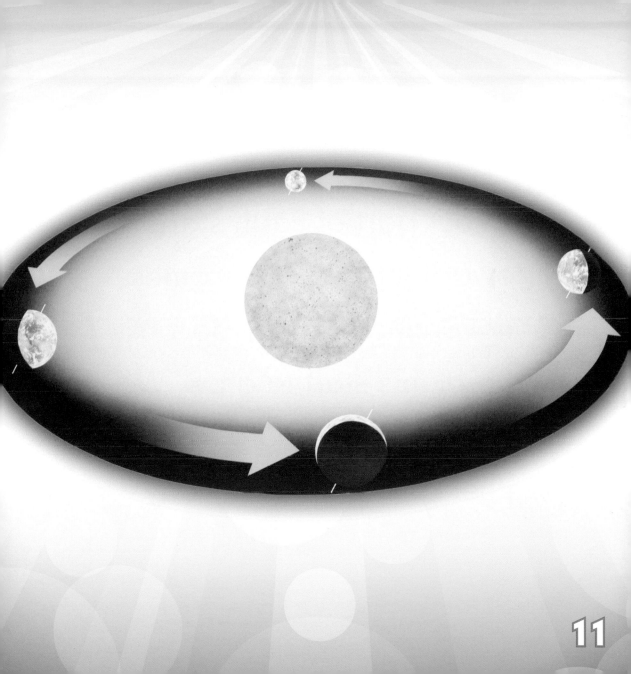

## Spring

When our part of Earth starts to tilt toward the sun, it becomes spring. Spring is pretty because all the plants start to grow. We also start to have more sun! The weather gets nicer every day.

# Summer

After spring comes summer. When summer comes, our part of Earth is fully tilted toward the sun. Summer can be hot! The days get longer and the sun stays out all day. It's fun to play outside in summer!

# Fall

As Earth moves through its orbit, summer ends. Our part of Earth starts to tilt away from the sun. It changes to fall. The days get shorter, and we can feel it get cooler. The leaves on the trees turn red, orange, and yellow.

# Winter

Next comes winter, when our part of Earth tilts away from the sun. We have less sun in the winter than in other seasons. Days are cold and short, and nights are long. Some places get snow. Snow is very cold!

Can you guess what happens when winter ends? Spring comes again! After 1 year, Earth made one whole orbit around the sun. We had spring, summer, fall, and winter. What season do you like the best?

more
sunlight on
top half

summer

sun

sun

winter

less sunlight
on top half

21

# Glossary

**axis:** an imaginary line through Earth from the North Pole to the South Pole

**orbit:** to travel in a circle or oval around something, or the path used to make that trip

**position:** the place where a thing or person is

**tilt:** when something is positioned at an angle

# For More Information

## Books

Lin, Grace, and Ranida McKneally. *Our Seasons.* Watertown, MA: Charlesbridge Publishing, 2006.

Rockwell, Anne. *Four Seasons Make a Year.* New York, NY: Walker & Company, 2004.

## Websites

**The Revolution of the Earth Around Our Sun**
*www.kidsgeo.com/geography-for-kids/0019-the-revolution-of-the-earth.php*
Read and watch a video about our changing seasons.

**Seasons**
*education.nationalgeographic.com/education/multimedia/seasons/*
View a fun graphic about Earth's revolution around the sun!

# Index